MW01204160

Maasai Life
and
Christian Practice:
A Photographic Portfolio

Maasai Life
and
Christian Practice:
A Photographic Portfolio

by

Fred Foy Strang, Ph.D.

Eden Green, LLC

Maasai Life and Christian Practice: A Photographic Portfolio

Copyright © Fred Foy Strang, 2010

Published by:
Eden Green, LLC
505 Beachland Blvd., Suite 1
PMB # 264
Vero Beach, Florida 32963

Printed in the United States of America

All rights reserved according to the United States Copyright Act. No portion of this book in paper, electronic, or any other form may be reproduced, stored in a retrieval system, or transmitted in any form or by any means—electronic, mechanical, photocopy, recording, or any other. Limited, non-commercial academic and ecclesiastical usage with appropriate acknowledgement is allowed without permission.

Photographs of individuals were taken and are used with permission. To protect identity, any names included in the text are not actual names of persons depicted in photographs.

A percentage of any profit derived from the sale of this project is given for various assistance to the Maasai people through the Maasai Special Projects Fund, Inc., a 501(c)3 entity.

For information about the author and links to the work of the MSPF: http://web.me.com/fredfoystrang

Library of Congress Cataloging-in-Publication Data

Strang, Fred Foy

Maasai Life and Christian Practice: A Photographic Portfolio
by Fred Foy Strang

Summary: "An intriguing photographic record of traditional Maasai life and Christian influence in the 20th century, including a unique record of Maasai hand counting signs." –Provided by the publisher.

ISBN 13 : 978-0-578-05245-8

1. Maasai—Africa. 2. Photography—Maasai 3. Religious Life—Maasai Christian Worship. 4. Hand Counting Signs—Maasai.

ACKNOWLEDGEMENTS

The photographs and written material presented in this portfolio are, unless otherwise noted, my own. Duplication in any form without the permission of the author is forbidden with the exception of limited, non-commercial, non-published academic or ecclesiastical usage where authorship is duly noted. These photographs were taken with permission during periods of my missionary activity in Africa and largely represent Presbyterian Church of East Africa (PCEA) practice among the Maasai people. These images are representative of Maasai life and Christian practice at the end of the 20th century. While there are brief descriptions of the photographs, the project is primarily photographic in nature.

I would like to acknowledge and thank my colleague, Dr. T. Jack Thompson, for encouraging use of photography as a means to show practices of current Maasai life and Christian practice. In addition, thank you to the Maasai Special Projects Fund, Inc. and the Community Church of Vero Beach, Florida for financial assistance and to the many Maasai people who have so graciously allowed me to photograph them over the past 28 years. Finally, thank you to my family, *Naserian, Tadjeu,* and *Odo Mungi,* for your loving support throughout this and every project.

Ashe tEnkai ! Thanks be to God!

TAUTA
The Rev. Dr. Fred Foy Strang

The meat from your cow is not enough.

Maasai Proverb

Recorded by the author, 1982

Olosho-oibor, Kenya

CONTENTS

PREFACE

In the Great Rift Valley of Kenya and Tanzania, a proud tribe of nomadic herdsmen wander the dry brown scrub grass dotted with green acacia thorn trees. Their land is harsh, seared by soaring temperatures and driving winds. With cattle, goats, and sheep, they move their families in search of fresh grass and precious water. Their villages are arranged in circles. Their homes are made from dung. Their lifestyle is simple—yet their lives are filled with rich traditions and ceremony. In the epoch of modernization, they are a living witness to a vanishing culture. They call themselves Maasai.

I penned these words in 1982 when, as a young college student, I had my first encounter with Maasai people living in a Maasai village as a Presbyterian mission volunteer. My reaction then was much like that of others who have written about the Maasai—respect and admiration. For over 28 years now, I have had the privilege of working with Maasai people. This long-standing relationship affords a unique opportunity of understanding a distinctive culture and ever-changing influences. While I have traversed the breadth of Maasai territories in both Kenya and Tanzania, I spent the majority of my time in the Kajiado (*Olkejuado*, long river) district of Kenya and so have a much clearer picture of Maasai life among the clans, sections, and families occupying that geographical area.

The Maasai are a Nilo-Hamitic group of herds-people who live in East Africa, specifically in the countries of Kenya and Tanzania. Their origins have been a subject of lively academic and anthropological discussion. Some early writers claimed Semitic ancestry dating back over 5,000 years, but more recent scholarship points to a somewhat later migration from northern Africa. Millennia ago, a tall, slender group of Nilotes practiced hunting and gathering in the southern part of what is now Sudan. When knowledge of agriculture came through that region, the Nilotes tried their hand, but failed. Finding their true calling with animals, they became accomplished herds-people and moved southward seeking suitable lands for their livestock. Concurrently, in what is now Ethiopia, another people group took up agriculture and developed a terrace system. Known as the Megalithic Cushites for their expert stonework in terrace farming and Hamitic language, they also moved southward to the fertile highlands of Kenya.

Later, the Nilotes and Hamites intermarried resulting in a hybrid group which became known as the Maasai, a name referring to the speakers of their tribal language, *ol maa*. This synthesis can be readily observed in the Maasai practices of age-group divisions (Nilotic) and male circumcision and female clitoridectomy (Hamitic). In addition, the short bladed sword, flowing toga-like garment, and leather sandals used by modern Maasai are reminiscent of ancient Roman influences from a Northern African origin. So, the Maasai, an amalgam of Nile region Nilotes and a North African people speaking a Hamitic language, began a southward trek arriving near Lake Turkana about the 15th century A.D. subsequently settling into the fertile grazing plains of the Great Rift Valley before the arrival of European explorers.

Once a numerous and powerful group, the Maasai found themselves decimated by new diseases, moved from their best lands, and out of favor with both colonial and subsequent independent African governments. Over the years, they have been reluctant to give up their manner of life in exchange for sirens of modernity. From the onset of western foray into East Africa, the Church has played a part, for good and for ill, in the lives of many. In the scope of this work, I cannot delve into these matters, but offer this visual account of culture, change, and hope.

MAP OF MAASAI INHABITANCE

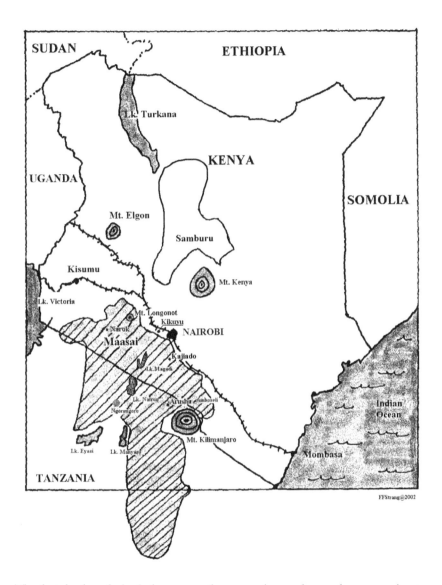

The hatched and shaded area on the map above shows the approximate habitation region of the Maasai people in Kenya and Tanzania.

Title: Two Maasai Villages

Date: 1882 and 1982

Location: Near *Longonot, Ewuaso Kedong,* Kenya

Photographer: Joseph Thomson, Fred Foy Strang

Description:

A historic, traditional village, one in which many Maasai live today, (s: *enkang,* pl: *ekangi*) is a family group living together in a community. This affords the advantage of sharing labor among many, added protection, and an enjoyable, communal life. These homes are low, oblong, stick-framed structures coated with a mixture of dung and mud. Inside there is a room for small animals leading on to a larger room with several cow hide covered bed areas. The only ventilation is from the main door and a few small holes in the exterior wall that are most often kept plugged with a cloth or skin.

The photographic pair of traditional Maasai homes is a fascinating reminder of an enduring way of life. In the first photograph, explorer Joseph Thomson provides a lithograph of a Maasai village near Mount *Longonot* in the *Ewuaso Kedong* from his expedition of 1882; below it, a photograph taken by the writer in the very same area in 1982. Although the time between the images spans one hundred years, the scenes are virtually the same (Joseph Thomson, *Through Masai Land,* London: Sampson, Low, Marston, Searle and Rivington, 1885, 418).

Title: Maasai Elder at *Olosho-oibor*

Date: 1982

Location: *Olosho-oibor*, Kenya

Photographer: Fred Foy Strang

Description:

This image was made at the village of *Olosho-oibor* beneath the stately *Ngong* Hills. The Maasai elder depicted in the photograph was the leader of his family and a very well respected man. His fading hair is indicative of both many years in the African sun and his advancement in years. He wears the typical blanket wrap employed by elders as both a sign of their age group and as a practical barrier against the scaring heat of the sun during the day and the cool, forceful valley wind at night. His ears are pierced in the traditional fashion with simple, but handsome bead adornment. This particular elder had a problem with vision in his right eye.

Title: Elders at *Saikeri*

Date: 1982

Location: *Saikeri*, Kenya

Photographer: Fred Foy Strang

Description:

This image was made at *Saikeri* in the *Ewuaso Kedong* area of the Rift Valley west of the Ngong Hills in Kenya. The elders pictured were assembled to hear a Presbyterian (PCUSA) missionary's request to hold a service of Christian baptism for new Maasai Christians in their village. After some deliberation and discussion with other leaders from the village, the elders granted the request.

This photograph captures the patriarchal order of Maasai society which remains a respected and functioning structure today. The missionary was wise to follow tribal protocol in asking the elder's permission prior to administering the sacrament of baptism. To do otherwise would have been viewed as blatant disrespect and could have undermined future missionary endeavors in the area. These elders all have traditional ear cuttings and ornamentation and wear blankets as both symbols of their office and for warmth in the windy evenings. The man in the center is using a fly whisk fashioned from a zebra or wildebeest tail. An example of the small wooden seats (*olorika*) on which the men sit and preside can be seen on the right of the photograph.

Title: *Oloiboni* near *Oldanyati*

Date: 1989

Location: Near *Oldanyati, Kenya*

Photographer: Fred Foy Strang

Description:

An important way in which Maasai interact with *Enkai* (God) is through the work of the tribe's spiritual and ceremonial leader, *oloiboni*, the loibon. The *oloiboni* is a ritual expert and a diviner who comes into the position through family genealogy. There can be several *iloibonok* practicing among different Maasai clans simultaneously. The *oloiboni* is considered a mediator between *Enkai* and the people and is an important part of any ceremonial activity in traditional Maasai society. This photograph was taken by request at a ceremony in the vicinity of the village of *Oldanyati*. The occasion was a special ceremony of reconciliation (*Asiei Onker*—The Work of the Ram) between family groups to restore peace after the occurrence of a serious injustice. The photograph depicts a respected *oloiboni* carefully watching over the complex ceremony. His cleanly shaved head is the mark of a rite of purification conducted before the ceremony. He sits with authority on a three-legged stool (*olorika*), wrapped in a red blanket, a favorite color and pattern of the *Keekonyokie* clan.

Title: Warrior at *Olosho-oibor*

Date: 1982

Location: *Olosho-oibor*, Kenya

Photographer: Fred Foy Strang

Description:

Part of being a Maasai man is going through the warrior stage of life. The warrior pictured is part of the *Keekonyokie* warrior group which was active in 1982. The band of warriors came to our village one day with great ceremony--singing, dancing, and jumping for the entire village. They were invited by the village elders to stay for a special meal after which they were given some animals to take back to their own special warrior village (*manyata*). Historically, the warriors have been a vital part of the order of Maasai society and continue to be held in high regard in spite of colonial and African independent government's attempts to disband the practice.

This image shows a resplendent Maasai warrior, tall and proud. His beadwork is of fine quality and may be the work of his mother or certainly a relative in his home village. His ears are cut and adorned in the traditional fashion, but this warrior has looped his left ear lobe up and over the top of his ear for additional visual impact. He also has intentional facial scarring near his right and left temple as well as on his arm--both signs of bravery and tolerance of pain. The short sword (*olalem*) in its scabbard at his hip and the fighting club (*oringa*) in his left hand are typical equipment carried and used by a warrior.

Title: Warriors Dancing at *Olosho-oibor*

Date: 1982

Location: *Olosho-oibor*, Kenya

Photographer: Fred Foy Strang

Description:

    This photograph of the previously mentioned *Keekonyokie* warrior group captures the essence of warrior dancing. The ecstatic dance is portrayed in the facial expression of the warriors. In this particular dance, the men circled round and round each other, swaying and thrusting out their chests and heads while rhythmically chanting. As the song began to reach its pinnacle, the warriors began to jump while a lead, higher-pitched voice sang over the rhythmic vocals. The words of praise concern the great deeds of this group, particularly the one jumping.

    Although the black and white image cannot covey the hues, brilliant red ochre coats each man's hair and, in traditional *Keekonyokie* dress, each wears predominantly red cloth and beads. Most of the men have two sticks: a thin herding or walking stick *(engudi)* and a darker, multi-purpose stick *(esiare narok)*. One of the men in the foreground has a fly whisk *(ol kidongoi)*. All the warriors pictured have on modern shoes of some sort as opposed to leather sandals indicating their proximity to trading areas in *Ngong*, *Kiserian*, and *Olepolos*.

Title: Warriors Playing *Enkeshei*

Date: 1988

Location: Near *Najile*, Kenya

Photographer: Fred Foy Strang

Description:

The following photograph shows a group of warriors enjoying a game called *enkeshei* (or *bao*, borrowed from the Swahili word for "wood" and referring to the wooden playing board). *Enkeshei* is a fast-paced game of strategy where the object is to take the stones of one's opponent by landing in juxtaposition to him on a board (or the ground) with parallel indentations. In some areas, the men refer to the stones as *enkishu* (cattle) and the object becomes capturing the opponent's herd!

Maasai are also generally quick witted and enjoy a good prank. Laughter at folk stories and jokes is common around evening fires in villages and in Maasai gatherings at trading centers, cattle markets, and Christian church fellowship activities.

Title: Maasai Boy

Date: 1989

Location: Near *Saikeri*, Kenya

Photographer: Fred Foy Strang

Description:

This young Maasai herd's boy was photographed in his village near *Saikeri* after bringing the animals home from a day of grazing. His ears have been cut, but are still being stretched as evidenced by the two wooden blocks inserted in the lobes. He wears the simple cloth of a young man and carries the herding stick (*engudi*) which are typical accoutrements of this stage of his life, that of between being young boy and junior warrior.

Of interesting note is his age-mate cousin (not pictured, but just to one side) who attends school. Both young men are of the same Maasai family, in the same age group, and live in the same village; however, the one is in training to become a junior warrior while the other hopes to have a job in the city. These young men are growing up experiencing two vastly different situations. The value of history and tradition, the forces of change, and the reality of modernization create a climate of tension and challenge for the Maasai. Most Maasai people living in the geographic areas represented in these photographs exist in a delicate and difficult position between the two worlds of traditional, historic Maasai culture and contemporary Africa.

Title: Maasai Woman at *Olosho-oibor*

Date: 1988

Location: *Olosho-oibor*, Kenya

Photographer: Fred Foy Strang

Description:

This photograph depicts a Christian woman from a very traditional Maasai family. The image conveys some of the reasons why this particular woman is considered a great beauty. At certain periods of life, Maasai women may shave their heads. This is also seen as an attractive feature. This woman is healthy, as can be noted by her full face and broad shoulders. Health is of vital importance to survive and thrive in the harsh environment of the Rift Valley. On close inspection, one can note the intricate, circular scars on the face. These circular patterns were made at a young age by a traditional tattoo technique and can be considered one of the finest examples in existence. Finally, this woman is a master beadworker (*esiaai isaen*). While her adornment in this photograph is simple, it is of superior quality. Her beadwork is highly sought out and always fetches the top market price. Even today, she teaches the craft to younger generations and is also often called upon to make specialized ceremonial pieces.

Title: Maasai Beadworkers and Beadwork

Date: 1989 & 1998

Location: *Ngong Hills*, Kenya

Photographer: Fred Foy Strang

Description:

Some Maasai women are experts in the art of beadwork and market their product with panache in Nairobi and other places. This scene shows two Maasai women sitting to do their beadwork on the floor of a more modern wood and tin home. These particular women are professing Christians and members of a local PCEA congregation. They use the monies secured from their beadwork sales to fund the education of their children, improve their homes, purchase items at the market, and support activities in their church such as the Women's Guild. An additional image below is a representative sampling of Maasai beadwork items in use in the late 1990's.

Title: Maasai Woman at *Saikeri*

Date: 1989

Location: *Saikeri*, Kenya

Photographer: Fred Foy Strang

Description:

      This is a striking image of a Maasai woman with full bead adornment, chosen as this book's cover image. The occasion of the photograph was a church service at *Saikeri*. The woman was attending the service with other women and children to observe the Christian service. Of special note in this picture is the rich array of bead work. Maasai women do not wear this amount of beads on a daily basis, but reserve such a display for special ceremonies and events. Because Christian worship is considered an important ceremony to the community as a whole, Maasai women often don their best. Traditionally, beadwork assists in the performance of music and dance, thus beadwork is worn not only for beauty, but it is also an important part of indigenous music. The beads and bangles bounce and jingle in time with the women's rhythmic movements.

Title: PCEA Evangelists at *Olooseos*

Date: 1989

Location: *Olooseos*, Kenya

Photographer: Fred Foy Strang

Description:

    This photograph was taken at the *Olooseos* parish center, the Church of the Good Shepherd, the only stone church in the area. Fifteen Maasai were trained and commissioned as official PCEA lay evangelists. At the conclusion of their training, each evangelist received a bicycle to assist them in their itinerate ministry in the large parish. Of special interest is the fact that all the evangelists are in western dress. At the time of this photograph, the PCEA governing body for this parish was requiring leaders to wear western dress at all church functions. This policy has since been altered to either western dress or full traditional dress. In addition, there was one woman trained as an evangelist. As part of the PCEA Women's Guild, she wears head covering to all church functions.

    The evangelists play a key role in the PCEA effort among the Maasai. There are very few pastors assigned to the Maasai area, so the evangelists are responsible for the daily work and week-to-week services of several churches. An ordained pastor comes only occasionally to administer the sacraments or deal with a conflict. Without the evangelists, the work of the PCEA in Maasai churches would be severely crippled.

Title: PCEA Evangelists and Choir at *Olentoko*

Date: 1988

Location: *Olentoko*, Kenya

Photographer: Fred Foy Strang

Description:

    Olentoko is located in the *Ewuaso Kedong* Valley at the foot of Mount Suswa (*Oldoinyo Onyokie*). In the early 1980's, there was practically no Christian presence in the area, but by the late 1980's several villages had responded to the Christian gospel through the efforts of Maasai evangelists. This photograph depicts the first choir of the *Olentoko* church with the two evangelists, standing together on the left, who worked to evangelize the area. One of these evangelists has gone on for seminary training and become the only full-time, PCEA ordained Maasai clergy in the parish. The man in western dress on the right is a local church leader. The choir members are all dressed in their finest for Sunday worship.

    Although there have been various times of turmoil, the area at the eastern foot of Mount Suswa has been a strong PCEA Maasai area with at least six congregations, several evangelists, and a manse for the pastor 's visits. The *Olentoko* church sold animals to enable their evangelists to make an evangelistic preaching trip into Tanzania. This photograph offers testimony to the beginnings of PCEA Christian faith near Mount Suswa.

39

Title: PCEA Evangelist and Mother

Date: 1989

Location: *Olodungoro*, Kenya

Photographer: Fred Foy Strang

Description:

This image is one of contrasts and depicts the ongoing struggle between church and culture. The man is one of the PCEA commissioned evangelists, the woman is his mother. The evangelist had recently concluded the warrior period of his life; in fact, on my first encounter with him, I found him in full warrior dress. His mother, also a Christian, maintains her traditional dress and manner of life in spite of the changes around her. The evangelist was particularly proud of his new suit of bright blue material and wanted a photograph taken.

How will the Presbyterian Church of East Africa and the Christian Church in general deal with cultures such as those of the Maasai people? There are no easy answers. For evangelization and Christian growth among the Maasai, a cautious, culturally informed and respectful approach is vital.

Title: PCEA *Olodungoro*

Date: 1989

Location: *Olodungoro*, Kenya

Photographer: Fred Foy Strang

Description:

Like *Olentoko*, *Olodungoro* is located in the *Ewuaso Kedong* Valley near Mount Suswa, but further removed. This photograph is of the church building, leadership, and part of the congregation gathered for Sunday worship. Those in western dress are evangelists or local leaders who would own suits for attending Kirk session meetings. Books held by two people are New Testament portions in the Maasai language, while the notebooks held by the kneeling evangelists are used to write the order of worship and record attendance and offering amounts.

The tin building is a typical example of remote church building construction-- buried posts supporting a simple roof design, all covered with tin sheets, wooden window openings for light and ventilation, and a dirt floor. A water tank can be seen on the right rear of the photograph which, in season, provides drinking water from roof run-off. The policy of the Kenyan government at the time of this photograph was to provide a primary school teacher if a community could provide a building for instruction and housing for the teacher. Continuing its historic commitment to education, the PCEA built churches of this type to include a room at the rear of the building which was to be used on Sundays as a church office and during the week as housing for the teacher. The PCEA evangelist would work closely with the teacher to provide weekly Bible instruction for attending Maasai school children.

Title: PCEA New Church Development at *Eluai*

Date: 1988

Location: *Eluai*, Kenya

Photographer: Fred Foy Strang

Description:

  Eluai is a small area at the southern foot of the *Ngong* Hills comprising several villages. A PCEA evangelist worked with a local Christian leader to establish a new church. Although the local leader is not a trained, commissioned, or paid PCEA evangelist, he undertook leading two PCEA churches in the area. His serious commitment is typical of Christian leaders in many areas where neither evangelists nor pastors can be present.

  After initial evangelism efforts, a worship meeting place was selected and several seats and benches were constructed. In addition, a lectern was made out of a small acacia tree. Sunday worship meetings continued at this outdoor sanctuary until numbers grew sufficiently to raise funds needed for construction of a church building. This numerical growth included a number of men, who, having control of the village livestock, sold animals for the project.

Title: First Service at PCEA *Kimuka*

Date: 1982

Location: *Kimuka*, Kenya

Photographer: Fred Foy Strang

Description:

      This photograph is of the assembling of the congregation for the first service of Christian worship at the new *Kimuka* PCEA church building. Like *Eluai*, the congregation at *Kimuka* had meet under an acacia tree for a protracted period until membership and funds were sufficient to construct a permanent building. An American PCUSA missionary is pictured in the far right along with several Presbyterian college students from the New Wilmington Missionary Conference, Pennsylvania who assisted in the construction of the church.

      Several children and young people are seen in school dress indicating the availability and acceptance of the school on the hill towards *Ngong*, a long established trading center. The women in the center are of Kikuyu origin and married to Maasai men. The presence of the Kikuyu in this area was beginning to be more pronounced as Maasai at the foot of the *Ngong* Hills were practicing farming in addition to their traditional herding activities. The PCEA *Kimuka* church has held services in both Maasai and Swahili languages throughout its history giving evidence of Kikuyu influence in this Maasai region of the Rift Valley.

Title: Groundbreaking at PCEA *Olcani*

Date: 1999

Location: Up the Hill from *Olosho-oibor*, Kenya

Photographer: Fred Foy Strang

Description:

A PCEA pastor and evangelist offered prayers at the groundbreaking of a new church on the *Ngong* Hills, *Olcani*. The word *olcani* in the Maasai language means "tree" and is associated with medicine and healing. The church derived its name from the beautiful acacia tree which will be at its entrance and the theological significance of the Gospel's healing power in the lives of people. The population of the *Ngong* Hills has increased dramatically with government land divisions and the Maasai's subsequent selling of many acres of land to other people groups who want to farm the rich bottom land at the foot of the mountain.

The Maasai have a proverb that indicates the challenge churches like *Oclani* face: *Merep enkaboboki o lcani likai cani*. "The bark of one tree will not stick to another tree." In other words, people of one ethnicity cannot absorb the lifestyle and culture of another. With the influx of various tribal groups into the areas which have traditionally been inhabited solely by Maasai, Christian people of various tribal backgrounds will have to come to terms with their differences and accept one another in the spirit of Christian kinship (Galatians 3:28).

Title: Maasai Christian Youth Fellowship (MCYF)

Date: 1989

Location: *Olosho-oibor*, Kenya

Photographer: Fred Foy Strang

Description:

   This photograph shows the Maasai Christian Youth Fellowship (MCYF) engaged in a time of praise and worship in the village of *Olosho-oibor*. The houses are a ferro-cement prototype with concrete floors and raised, vented fireplaces arranged in a traditional village manner. The Caucasian woman is the author's wife, PCUSA missionary Cecily Strang, R.N., who lived with the Maasai at *Olosho-oibor* with her family. The MCYF was formed by Maasai young people as a NGO (non-governmental organization) with the purpose of evangelization of Maasai people. At the time of this photograph, the MCYF would meet weekly for Bible study, worship, and fellowship. Three or four times annually, they would conduct an "outreach," traveling to remote areas for weeks of preaching and teaching. As a non-denominational NGO, the MCYF worked with pastors and evangelists of various denominations to connect new converts with churches nearby.

   The Maasai young people in this photograph are wearing western-style clothes indicative of their school attendance or their employment in one of the nearby towns. The use of guitar and upraised hands of several indicate beginning trends among young people to accept more expressive forms of worship within the context of traditionally rigid denominational backgrounds. In 1998, the MCYF was given a camp property on the *Ngong* Hills, Camp *Mwamba* (rock: Swahili), as a Christian leadership training center and youth retreat facility.

Title: MCYF Showing the Jesus Film at *Olepolos*

Date: 1988

Location: *Olepolos*, Kenya

Photographer: Fred Foy Strang

Description:

    This image is representative of a typical showing of the "Jesus Film" by the MCYF as part of their regular "outreach" events. The showing of the film was always held at night well after the cattle had been secured in the villages. If possible, the film was shown in a school room or church building. In more remote areas, there were many occasions where a large sheet was strung between trees as a screen and the film shown outside. Electricity was provided by a portable generator. A kerosene lamp can be noted on the projection table to assist film reel changes. The audio of the film was in the Maasai language and always impressed audiences.

    After the film, members of the MCYF would give their Christian testimonies, sing, preach, and give an opportunity for anyone to receive Jesus Christ as their Lord. On the occasion of this photograph, seventeen people came forward to renounce sin and profess Christian faith.

Title: PCEA *Olosho-oibor* Choir

Date: 1989

Location: *Olosho-oibor*, Kenya

Photographer: Cecily Strang (used by permission)

Description:

This photograph is of the choir at the PCEA *Olosho-oibor* church. This Sunday was the first day the choir had robes. Prior to this day, a majority of the choir wore traditional clothing. The purchase of the robes was initiated by the African leadership of the congregation some time after participating in a Presbytery event at the parish center, *Olooseos*, where several choirs from nearby towns had matching choir robes.

The *Olosho-oibor* church was the first PCEA congregation in the Rift Valley and the first permanent church building constructed. The building is well constructed with wood siding, a metal roof, and a finished cement floor. The congregation has its own communion vessels (pictured in the center of the table) which were given by a congregation in Florida. Having their own communion trays allows the congregation to serve the sacrament of the Lord's Supper whenever an ordained minister visits. The sterling silver trays and the choir robes are additions which indicate continued outside influence on indigenous expressions of Maasai Christian worship.

Title: Maasai Deaconess Preparing Communion

Date: 1989

Location: Near *Najile*, Kenya

Photographer: Fred Foy Strang

Description:

   This Maasai Christian woman is a health care worker at the Maasai Rural Development Center at *Olooseos*, member of the Maasai Christian Youth Fellowship, and PCEA deaconess. Shown here, the deaconess is preparing the sacrament of Holy Communion for distribution at an outdoor PCEA worship service at *Najile* near Mount Suswa in the *Ewuaso Kedong* Valley.

   The significance of the image is the contrast between the rural isolation of the worship setting and the formalness of the communion vessel and the woman's dress. This contrast could indicate a high respect for the sacraments and the act of worship, it may be indicative of outside influence on Maasai Christian culture, or perhaps the reality is that it is a bit of both.

Title: PCEA *Najile*

Date: 1999

Location: *Najile*, Kenya

Photographer: Fred Foy Strang

Description:

This photograph is of the congregation gathering for worship at the PCEA *Najile* church building. The previously mentioned teacher's room is clearly visible as an addition on the right side of the church building. Although in a remote area, this church building has a cement floor like the *Olosho-oibor* church. The escarpment leading down into the *Ewuaso Kedong* Valley is visible in the background.

Many of the women gathered are in traditional Maasai dress. The area's PCEA Maasai pastor is visible in a clerical collar and jacket below the left eave of the building. This pastor encourages people to wear traditional Maasai clothes to worship if that is what they normally wear at their home. This is a marked change in policy towards Maasai people from that of the early 1980's.

Najile has grown into a rural trading center and has a well established boarding school which is located near the church building. The congregations of *Najile*, *Olodungoro*, and *Olentoko* are in the process of building a stone manse just behind the *Najile* church for a pastor so that he can remain in the valley area with his family while conducting his ministry to parish churches.

Title: First Baptism at *Saikeri*

Date: 1982

Location: *Saikeri*, Kenya

Photographer: Fred Foy Strang

Description:

    This photograph conveys the essence of Jesus' Great Commission (Matthew 28:16-20). A PCEA evangelist and an American PCUSA missionary had followed the heels of a water project development at *Saikeri* with a prolonged and culturally sensitive evangelism effort. This evangelist and several other Christian leaders had been warriors and knew proper protocol as well as effective means for communicating the message of Jesus Christ. After much investment of time in building relationships with people in the village, one of the elders agreed that his family would be baptized. This service was significant as the whole family was baptized following the elder's leadership and Biblical precedent ("Believe in the Lord Jesus Christ, and you will be saved--you and your household." Acts 16:31).

    The woman pictured in the center is the elder's first wife who watches with joy as one of her children is baptized by the PCUSA missionary. Assisting in the service and holding the baptismal water is the area's PCEA commissioned evangelist. This worship service marked the first Christian baptism in the area.

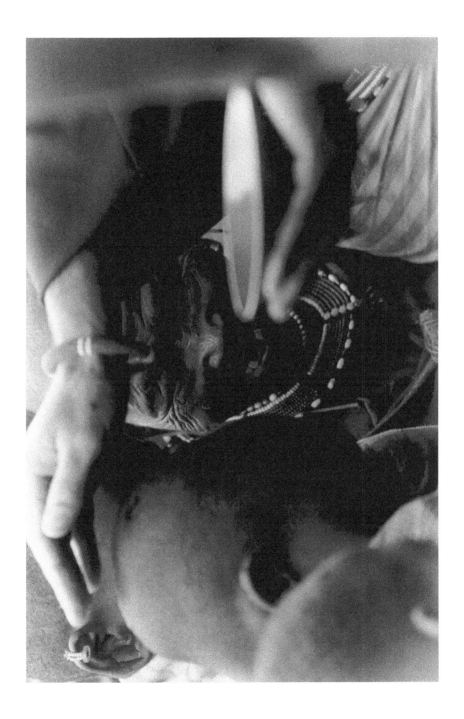

Title: Second Baptism at *Saikeri*

Date: 1988

Location: *Saikeri*, Kenya

Photographer: Cecily Strang (used by permission)

Description:

This photograph records the second PCEA baptism at *Saikeri*. In the six years between the first *Saikeri* baptism and this photograph, a church building had been constructed and a PCEA evangelist appointed. Utilizing materials and training he had received at the *Enkomono loo Evangelists* (Fellowship of the Evangelists) training program, the evangelist recruited and prepared a sizeable number to receive Christian baptism. The location of a government-sponsored primary school at *Saikeri* assured that there were many children in the area. At this particular service, 69 persons were baptized.

The Caucasian male on the left is the author, PCUSA missionary Rev. Dr. Fred Foy Strang. The *Saikeri* PCEA evangelist is standing next to me. On the far right is the writer's son, Jesse Strang, who is held by a member of the Maasai Christian Youth Fellowship.

Title: Concluding a Worship Service at AIC *Oreteti*

Date: 1999

Location: Corner *Baridi*, Kenya

Photographer: Fred Foy Strang

Description:

      This photograph is a typical panorama of the setting of Maasai Christian worship. The location is at the African Inland Church (AIC), *Oreteti* at the southern end of the *Ngong* Hills facing south into the Rift Valley towards Magadi. The Caucasians on the left are the Strang family. Jesse (*Tadjeu*), pictured in the previous photograph as a little boy, is shown here as a tall young man. It is customary in many Maasai churches to conclude worship by gathering outside of the building in a circle for a final hymn and prayer (Matthew 26:30, Mark 14:26). After this conclusion, people enjoy a time of Christian fellowship before walking back to their villages.

Let the peoples praise you, O God;

Let all the peoples praise you.

Let the nations be glad and sing for joy.

Psalm 67:3-4

Title: Ecstatic Maasai Christian Worship

Date: 1995

Location: New Church Development, *Ewuaso Kedong*, Kenya

Photographer: Fred Foy Strang

Description:

The image portrays Maasai men and women gathered in close proximity expressing heart-felt worship at a Christian service. After a protracted service of blessing a new plot of land given for the construction of a new PCEA church building, a lengthy time of singing ensued. The singing was marked by *indungetta* (choruses) rather than traditional western hymnody and engaged both young and old, male and female. The *indungetta* are an emerging distinctive in Maasai Christian worship as they employ indigenous musical forms with original lyrics of relevantly articulated faith.

At this service, the women swayed and rocked and the men jumped and danced. At the point of the making of this image, men and women had converged into the center of the outdoor meeting space and, as the song concluded, erupted in a spontaneous cacophony of prayer. This prayer time was very emotional and lasted upwards of thirty minutes. As the energy waned, those gathered gradually dispersed to their places for the continuation of the service.

Title: Spraying Cattle near *Saikeri*

Date: 1999

Location: *Saikeri*, Kenya

Photographer: Fred Foy Strang

Description:

      In this photograph, two Maasai men take care of their cattle at an animal watering area near *Saikeri*. Their traditional clothing is indicative of many Maasai who engage in animal husbandry, even in modern times. The men are using a hand pump sprayer to douse their animals with an insecticidal bath for ticks. Unprotected by this modern medicine, most animals quickly succumb to various blood borne disease and either become too sickly for use or die. The hand pump sprayer is an appropriate technological tool as it has limited, user serviceable parts and is extremely reliable. The insecticide is mixed in an open bucket with the draw-tube inserted therein. The man on the left is pumping the hand-operated plunger, while the man on the right operates the spray wand to soak each animal. In the foreground, a simple acacia thorn enclosure keeps a particular group of animals contained for their bath. Upon completion, this group of cattle is released and another set is herded in for treatment. This process continues until the entire herd has received a dosage. Maasai in the *Saikeri* region are fortunate that a dam holding rainwater from the previous season provides not only drinking water for people and animals, but enough to spare for this important *olcani*, the Maasai reference for medicinal treatment.

Title: Counting Sheep at *Asiei Onker*

Date: 1989

Location*:*   Near *Oldanyati*, Kenya

Photographer: Fred Foy Strang

Description:

The *Asiei Onker* (The Work of the Ram) ceremony is an important rite to restore order after a grievous act has caused conflict between family groups or clans. In this case, a person had been killed. While it was the lesser crime of manslaughter, the damage of loosing a family member, especially a man in the prime of his life, was causing increasing strife between two families. The *oloiboni* was called in to direct and oversee a complex ceremony of reconciliation.

As this rite involved the exchange of animals, one aspect of the proceeding became obviously important, the quantity of each type of animal brought to pay for the debt. In this image, the man on the far right is the father of the one who was killed and immediately next to him is the *oloiboni*. Both these men, along with the others present, are inspecting both the quality and sufficiency of this herd of sheep. While the man at the far left in the back appears to be writing down information, all those involved were not only saying aloud numbers, but utilizing a unique method of hand counting symbols which could be readily seen by everyone. This was an important confirmation of the spoken number of animals to the large group of participants just outside the camera's view as the various herds were noisy and many other Maasai were talking.

MAASAI COUNTING

Maasai people have a unique way of counting and articulating numbers. Not only are there words for each number, but there is a corresponding hand signal. It has been suggested in conversations I have had with various Maasai people that these hand signals developed, at least in part, to facilitate honesty in buying, selling, and trading animals. Because Maasai life is so communal in nature, it is natural for animal commerce to be carried out in a public forum as well. By utilizing words as well as hand signals, there could be no confusion about price or quantity, even over the noise of other conversations and herds of animals. In addition, counting hand signals offer an example of the expressive nature of Maasai life and culture.

The right hand is normally used to form the signals. Each hand signal is done simultaneously with the saying of the corresponding word for the number. For instance, as one says *"nabo,"* the right hand, index finger pointed and pivoting at the wrist, is travelling downward to a stopping position even with the forearm and perpendicular to the upper arm. It will be noted that for most of the numbers greater than ten a hand signal similar to the corresponding one's place numeral is used. There is, however, then a bounce added to the hand movement or a doubling of the signal to distinguish these numbers from their one's place counterpart. In order to express a number with both a ten's place and a one's place numeral, the tens place numeral is said and signed followed by the saying and signing of the one's place numeral. For instance for the number 21 (*tikitam obo*), one says *"tikitam"* with the right arm extended upward perpendicular to the ground and the fingers snapping down to the palm two times followed immediately by saying *"obo,"* using the physical sign for *nabo* described above.

Nabo (one)

With the index finger pointed, the hand, pivoting at the wrist, moves downward and stops even with the arm.

Aare (two)

With the index and middle fingers extended and the other fingers held to the palm with the thumb, the index and middle fingers are wiggled back and forth.

Uni (three)

The index finger is held straight with the thumb alongside touching it about halfway down while the middle finger bends and is pulled in towards the hand. The ring and little fingers are bent and held close to the palm. The entire hand is then twisted back and forth in a motion parallel to the arm.

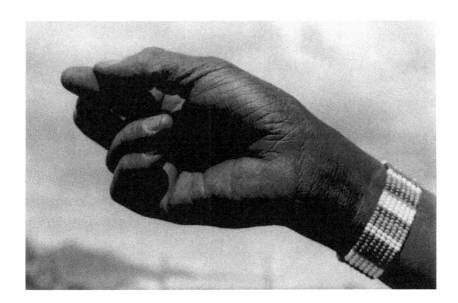

Onguan (four)

The index and middle fingers are extended and held together. The thumb holds the ring and little fingers bent in to the palm. Pivoting at the wrist, the hand moves downward and stops even with the arm.

Imiet (five)

A loose fist is made with the thumb protruding between the index and middle fingers. The hand is rotated to the outside of the body so that the palm faces slightly upward.

Ile (six)

With the index, middle, and ring fingers loosely extended, the thumb grasps the inward bent little finger. The little finger is then flicked outward one time.

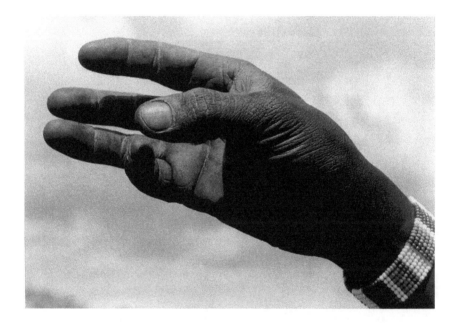

Naapishana (seven)

This motion is similar to the number one, but with subtle differences. The index finger is extended, the thumb rests on top of the other fingers which are bent in towards the palm. The hand, pivoting at the wrist, moves downward and bounces or quivers at its stopping point.

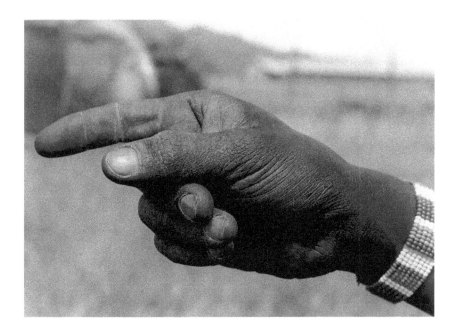

Isiet (eight)

The whole hand is opened with all fingers extended and is held rotated so that the palm is perpendicular to the ground. Again, the hand, pivoting at the wrist, makes a downward sweep.

Naaudo (nine)

The thumb and index finger are brought together in a circle similar to the international "O.K." sign. The hand is then swept downward as in previous signals.

Tomon (ten)

The forearm is bent at the elbow to become more perpendicular with the ground. The hand is held upright with fingers extended upward. Then, quickly, the fingers are all snapped forward to the palm one time. The photograph below is a view of the signal at its conclusion.

Tikitam (twenty)

The index finger is bent to join the thumb in a circle with the other fingers loosely extended. The index finger is snapped to its forward extension two times.

In-tomoni uni (thirty)

With the index finger extended and the thumb holding the other fingers bent in towards the palm, the hand, pivoting at the wrist, travels down to its natural stopping place two times. This signal is very similar to the number one.

Artam (forty)

The hand is held so that the open palm faces the ground (parallel) with all fingers extended and slightly apart. The hand is then wiggled side-to-side two times.

Onom (fifty)

A loose fist is made with the thumb protruding between the index and middle fingers. The hand is rotated to the outside of the body so that the palm faces slightly upward. To complete the signal for fifty, the hand is either rotated or bounced twice.

In-tomoni ile (sixty)

With the index, middle, and ring fingers loosely extended, the thumb grasps the inward bent little finger. The difference between the sign for sixty and the sign for six is that, for the larger number, the little finger is now flicked outward two times instead of once. There can also be some additional wrist movement for the higher number.

In-tomoni naapishana (seventy)

Similar to the signal for seven, the index finger is extended; the thumb rests loosely on top of the other fingers which are bent in towards the palm. The hand pivots at the wrist, moves downward and bounces and quivers several times. The difference between the smaller and larger numbers is in the amount of motion added to the signal.

In-tomoni isiet (eighty)

Similar to the number eight, the whole hand is opened with all fingers extended and is held so that the palm is roughly perpendicular to the ground. Again, the difference is in the amount of motion used. The hand makes a downward sweep and a slight wrist rotation is added for this higher number.

In-tomoni naaudo (ninety)

Like the signal for the number nine, the thumb and index finger are brought together to form a circle similar to the international "O.K." sign. Again, the difference is in the amount of motion used. For ninety, the hand is brought downward and, at the bottom of its sweep, is rotated at the wrist in a side-to-side, wiggling motion.

Iip (one hundred)

The forearm is bent at the elbow to become more perpendicular with the ground. The hand is held upright with all the fingers and thumb curled in like a loose fist. In one quick motion, the fingers and thumb are extended and the forearm moves slightly forward. The photographs below illustrate the two steps to this numeric signal.

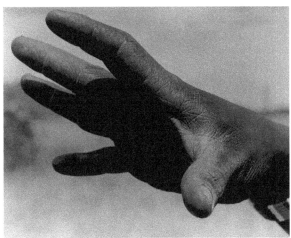

Title: Walking Proud

Date: 1999

Location: Near *Oloitokitok*, Kenya

Photographer: Fred Foy Strang

Description:

      This image of a solitary Maasai man walking through the bush at the base of Mt. Kilimanjaro epitomizes many assumptions and realities concerning Maasai people. Taken at the close of the 20th century, the photograph shows a man who takes care of his cattle, goats, and sheep, living in a manner similar to that of his grandfather and even generations prior. His magnificent beaded bracelet is a work of art. Upon closer inspection, he also wears a fine bead neck ornament. At his waist is the traditional short sword of Maasai warriors and herdsmen, *olalem*. He carries a stout herding stick, *esiare narok*, which is also useful as a weapon. The expanse of bush to each side, behind, and before this proud man is indicative of the harsh reality, but simple beauty of his life.

Everything has an end.

Maasai Proverb
Recorded by the author, 1982
Olosho-oibor, Kenya